Wilson Language Basics

Composition Book

Level 3

SECOND EDITION

Wilson Language Training Corporation

www.wilsonlanguage.com

www.fundations.com

Fundations® Student Composition Book 3

Item # F2STCBK3

ISBN 978-1-56778-508-1

SECOND EDITION

PUBLISHED BY:

Wilson Language Training Corporation
47 Old Webster Road
Oxford, MA 01540
United States of America

(800) 899-8454

www.wilsonlanguage.com

Printed in the U.S.A.

December 2018

① Sit *right*

Seat pulled in, feet on floor

LEFT-HANDED RIGHT-HANDED

② Place paper and hands *right*

Paper slanted, wrist straight, elbow on desk, other hand holding paper

LEFT-HANDED RIGHT-HANDED

③ Grip pencil *right*

Pencil held between index finger and thumb, resting on the other fingers

LEFT-HANDED RIGHT-HANDED

Let's *write!*

Sounds

1 ch, tch ✓   2 c, k, ck   3 m ✓   4 t ✓

Review Words

1 band ✓   2 stack ✓

3 clap. ✓   4 brunch ✓

Current Words

1 crunch ✓   2 pinch ✓

3 stretch   4 scrap

Sound Alike Words

1 right ✓   2 write ✓

Review Trick Words

1 should ✓   2 have ✓

Sentences

1 I think Dad said no.

_ to friend

2 Did your friend write to me?

Wilson Fundations® | ©2005, 2012 Wilson Language Training Corporation

Sounds

1 unk   2 c, k, ck   3 ch, tch   4 olt

Review Words

1 spring   2 lend

3 stump   4 stitch

Current Words

1 scold   2 jolt

3 mind   4 colt

Sound Alike Words

1 write   2 which

Review Trick Words

1 have   2 should

Sentences

1 The fox did not mind the cold.

2

Today's Date: _____   *Check-up* ☑

Sounds

1 c,k,ck   2 ch,tch   3 s,z   4 d,ed

Review Words

1 shock   2 craft

3 mind   4 watch

Current Words

1 catches   2 drummer

3 tripping   4 buggy

Sound Alike Words

1 guest   2 some

Review Trick Words

1 again   2 from

Sentences

1 Rick waxed the runners of the sled.

2 The man quickly splitting the logs.

Wilson Fundations® | ©2005, 2012 Wilson Language Training Corporation

Sounds

1 e-c, ed   2 ost   3 o-e   4 ive-t

Review Words

1 listed   2 shopper

3 flatness   4 confuse

Current Words

1 bravest   2 mojoed

3 mopping   4 inflatable

Sound Alike Words

1 mail   2 fined

Review Trick Words

1 school   2 something

Sentences

1 I scrapped my leg when I
hopped on the bus.

2

Sounds

1 i-e,i,y   2 îve   3 e-e,y   4 g

Review Words

1 construct   2 runner

3 exhale   4 deportable

Current Words

1 plenty   2 toboy

3 ftu   4 unit

Sound Alike Words

1 hi   2 high

Review Trick Words

1 animal   2 many

Sentences

1 We must protec the ozone.

2

Sounds

1 u, a, i   2 e-e, y, i   3 ive   4

Review Words

1 impact   2 stacks

3 contrast   4 dependable

Current Words

1 extra   2 imitate

3 studio   4

Sound Alike Words

1   2

Review Trick Words

1   2

Sentences

1

2

Sounds

1 c-c _y,e,i   2 u,a,i   3 z/s   4 r/j/y

Review Words

1 lazy   2 family

3 cry   4 empty

Current Words

1 studying   2 lazier

3 galaxies   4 emptiness

Sound Alike Words

1 flower   2 thrown

Review Trick Words

1 year   2 tomorrow

Sentences

1 My son is much happier.

2

Sounds

1 _____ 2 _____ 3 _____ 4 _____

Review Words

1 _____ 2 _____

3 _____ 4 _____

Current Words

1 _____ 2 _____

3 _____ 4 _____

Sound Alike Words

1 _____ 2 _____

Review Trick Words

1 _____ 2 _____

Sentences

1 _____

_____

2 _____

_____

Sounds

1 _____ 2 _____ 3 _____ 4 _____

Review Words

1 _____ 2 _____

3 _____ 4 _____

Current Words

1 _____ 2 _____

3 _____ 4 _____

Sound Alike Words

1 _____ 2 _____

Review Trick Words

1 _____ 2 _____

Sentences

1 _____

_____

2 _____

_____

Sounds

1 _____ 2 _____ 3 _____ 4 _____

Review Words

1 _____ 2 _____

3 _____ 4 _____

Current Words

1 _____ 2 _____

3 _____ 4 _____

Sound Alike Words

1 _____ 2 _____

Review Trick Words

1 _____ 2 _____

Sentences

1 _____

_____

2 _____

_____

Sounds

1 _____ 2 _____ 3 _____ 4 _____

Review Words

1 _____ 2 _____

3 _____ 4 _____

Current Words

1 _____ 2 _____

3 _____ 4 _____

Sound Alike Words

1 _____ 2 _____

Review Trick Words

1 _____ 2 _____

Sentences

1 _____

_____

2 _____

_____

Sounds

1 _____ 2 _____ 3 _____ 4 _____

Review Words

1 _____ 2 _____

3 _____ 4 _____

Current Words

1 _____ 2 _____

3 _____ 4 _____

Sound Alike Words

1 _____ 2 _____

Review Trick Words

1 _____ 2 _____

Sentences

1 _____

2 _____

Sounds

1   2   3   4

Review Words

1   2

3   4

Current Words

1   2

3   4

Sound Alike Words

1   2

Review Trick Words

1   2

Sentences

1

2

Today's Date: _____ *Check-up* ☐

Sounds

1 _____ 2 _____ 3 _____ 4 _____

Review Words

1 _____ 2 _____

3 _____ 4 _____

Current Words

1 _____ 2 _____

3 _____ 4 _____

Sound Alike Words

1 _____ 2 _____

Review Trick Words

1 _____ 2 _____

Sentences

1 _____

_____

2 _____

_____

Sounds

1   2   3   4

Review Words

1   2

3   4

Current Words

1   2

3   4

Sound Alike Words

1   2

Review Trick Words

1   2

Sentences

1

2

Today's Date: _____ *Check-up* ☐

Sounds

1 _____ 2 _____ 3 _____ 4 _____

Review Words

1 _____ 2 _____

3 _____ 4 _____

Current Words

1 _____ 2 _____

3 _____ 4 _____

Sound Alike Words

1 _____ 2 _____

Review Trick Words

1 _____ 2 _____

Sentences

1 _____

_____

2 _____

_____

Sounds

1 _____ 2 _____ 3 _____ 4 _____

Review Words

1 _____ 2 _____

3 _____ 4 _____

Current Words

1 _____ 2 _____

3 _____ 4 _____

Sound Alike Words

1 _____ 2 _____

Review Trick Words

1 _____ 2 _____

Sentences

1 _____

_____

2 _____

_____

Today's Date: _____ *Check-up* ☐

Sounds

1 _____ 2 _____ 3 _____ 4 _____

Review Words

1 _____ 2 _____

3 _____ 4 _____

Current Words

1 _____ 2 _____

3 _____ 4 _____

Sound Alike Words

1 _____ 2 _____

Review Trick Words

1 _____ 2 _____

Sentences

1 _____

_____

2 _____

_____

Sounds

1 _____ 2 _____ 3 _____ 4 _____

Review Words

1 _____ 2 _____

3 _____ 4 _____

Current Words

1 _____ 2 _____

3 _____ 4 _____

Sound Alike Words

1 _____ 2 _____

Review Trick Words

1 _____ 2 _____

Sentences

1 _____

_____

2 _____

_____

Sounds

1   2   3   4

Review Words

1   2

3   4

Current Words

1   2

3   4

Sound Alike Words

1   2

Review Trick Words

1   2

Sentences

1

2

Sounds

1 _____ 2 _____ 3 _____ 4 _____

Review Words

1 _____ 2 _____

3 _____ 4 _____

Current Words

1 _____ 2 _____

3 _____ 4 _____

Sound Alike Words

1 _____ 2 _____

Review Trick Words

1 _____ 2 _____

Sentences

1 _____

_____

2 _____

_____

Sounds

1 _____ 2 _____ 3 _____ 4 _____

Review Words

1 _____ 2 _____

3 _____ 4 _____

Current Words

1 _____ 2 _____

3 _____ 4 _____

Sound Alike Words

1 _____ 2 _____

Review Trick Words

1 _____ 2 _____

Sentences

1 _____

_____

2 _____

_____

Sounds

1   2   3   4

Review Words

1   2

3   4

Current Words

1   2

3   4

Sound Alike Words

1   2

Review Trick Words

1   2

Sentences

1

2

Sounds

1   2   3   4

Review Words

1   2

3   4

Current Words

1   2

3   4

Sound Alike Words

1   2

Review Trick Words

1   2

Sentences

1

2

Today's Date: _____ *Check-up* ☐

Sounds

1 _____ 2 _____ 3 _____ 4 _____

Review Words

1 _____ 2 _____

3 _____ 4 _____

Current Words

1 _____ 2 _____

3 _____ 4 _____

Sound Alike Words

1 _____ 2 _____

Review Trick Words

1 _____ 2 _____

Sentences

1 _____

2 _____

Today's Date: _____   *Check-up* ☐

Sounds

1 _____ 2 _____ 3 _____ 4 _____

Review Words

1 _____ 2 _____

3 _____ 4 _____

Current Words

1 _____ 2 _____

3 _____ 4 _____

Sound Alike Words

1 _____ 2 _____

Review Trick Words

1 _____ 2 _____

Sentences

1 _____

_____

2 _____

_____

Sounds

1   2   3   4

Review Words

1   2

3   4

Current Words

1   2

3   4

Sound Alike Words

1   2

Review Trick Words

1   2

Sentences

1

2

Sounds

1 _____ 2 _____ 3 _____ 4 _____

Review Words

1 _____ 2 _____

3 _____ 4 _____

Current Words

1 _____ 2 _____

3 _____ 4 _____

Sound Alike Words

1 _____ 2 _____

Review Trick Words

1 _____ 2 _____

Sentences

1 _____

_____

2 _____

_____

Sounds

1 _____ 2 _____ 3 _____ 4 _____

Review Words

1 _____ 2 _____

3 _____ 4 _____

Current Words

1 _____ 2 _____

3 _____ 4 _____

Sound Alike Words

1 _____ 2 _____

Review Trick Words

1 _____ 2 _____

Sentences

1

2

Sounds

1 _____ 2 _____ 3 _____ 4 _____

Review Words

1 _____ 2 _____

3 _____ 4 _____

Current Words

1 _____ 2 _____

3 _____ 4 _____

Sound Alike Words

1 _____ 2 _____

Review Trick Words

1 _____ 2 _____

Sentences

1 _____

_____

2 _____

_____

Check-up ☐

Sounds

1   2   3   4

Review Words

1   2

3   4

Current Words

1   2

3   4

Sound Alike Words

1   2

Review Trick Words

1   2

Sentences

1

2

Today's Date: _____ Check-up ☐

Sounds

1   2   3   4

Review Words

1   2

3   4

Current Words

1   2

3   4

Sound Alike Words

1   2

Review Trick Words

1   2

Sentences

1

2

Sounds

1 _____ 2 _____ 3 _____ 4 _____

Review Words

1 _____ 2 _____

3 _____ 4 _____

Current Words

1 _____ 2 _____

3 _____ 4 _____

Sound Alike Words

1 _____ 2 _____

Review Trick Words

1 _____ 2 _____

Sentences

1 _____

_____

2 _____

_____

Sounds

1   2   3   4

Review Words

1   2

3   4

Current Words

1   2

3   4

Sound Alike Words

1   2

Review Trick Words

1   2

Sentences

1

2

Sounds

1 _____ 2 _____ 3 _____ 4 _____

Review Words

1 _____ 2 _____

3 _____ 4 _____

Current Words

1 _____ 2 _____

3 _____ 4 _____

Sound Alike Words

1 _____ 2 _____

Review Trick Words

1 _____ 2 _____

Sentences

1 _____

2 _____

Today's Date: _____ *Check-up* ☐

Sounds

1 _____ 2 _____ 3 _____ 4 _____

Review Words

1 _____ 2 _____

3 _____ 4 _____

Current Words

1 _____ 2 _____

3 _____ 4 _____

Sound Alike Words

1 _____ 2 _____

Review Trick Words

1 _____ 2 _____

Sentences

1 _____

_____

2 _____

_____

Sounds

1   2   3   4

Review Words

1   2

3   4

Current Words

1   2

3   4

Sound Alike Words

1   2

Review Trick Words

1   2

Sentences

1

2

Sounds

1   2   3   4

Review Words

1   2

3   4

Current Words

1   2

3   4

Sound Alike Words

1   2

Review Trick Words

1   2

Sentences

1

2

Today's Date:

Check-up ☐

Sounds

1   2   3   4

Review Words

1   2

3   4

Current Words

1   2

3   4

Sound Alike Words

1   2

Review Trick Words

1   2

Sentences

1

2

Sounds

1 _____ 2 _____ 3 _____ 4 _____

Review Words

1 _____ 2 _____

3 _____ 4 _____

Current Words

1 _____ 2 _____

3 _____ 4 _____

Sound Alike Words

1 _____ 2 _____

Review Trick Words

1 _____ 2 _____

Sentences

1 _____

_____

2 _____

_____

Sounds

1 _____ 2 _____ 3 _____ 4 _____

Review Words

1 _____ 2 _____

3 _____ 4 _____

Current Words

1 _____ 2 _____

3 _____ 4 _____

Sound Alike Words

1 _____ 2 _____

Review Trick Words

1 _____ 2 _____

Sentences

1 _____

_____

2 _____

_____

Sounds

1   2   3   4

Review Words

1   2

3   4

Current Words

1   2

3   4

Sound Alike Words

1   2

Review Trick Words

1   2

Sentences

1

2

Sounds

1   2   3   4

Review Words

1   2

3   4

Current Words

1   2

3   4

Sound Alike Words

1   2

Review Trick Words

1   2

Sentences

1

2

Sounds

1   2   3   4

Review Words

1   2

3   4

Current Words

1   2

3   4

Sound Alike Words

1   2

Review Trick Words

1   2

Sentences

1

2

Sounds

1 _____ 2 _____ 3 _____ 4 _____

Review Words

1 _____ 2 _____

3 _____ 4 _____

Current Words

1 _____ 2 _____

3 _____ 4 _____

Sound Alike Words

1 _____ 2 _____

Review Trick Words

1 _____ 2 _____

Sentences

1 _____

_____

2 _____

_____

Sounds

1 _____ 2 _____ 3 _____ 4 _____

Review Words

1 _____ 2 _____

3 _____ 4 _____

Current Words

1 _____ 2 _____

3 _____ 4 _____

Sound Alike Words

1 _____ 2 _____

Review Trick Words

1 _____ 2 _____

Sentences

1 _____

_____

2 _____

_____

Sounds

1 _____ 2 _____ 3 _____ 4 _____

Review Words

1 _____ 2 _____

3 _____ 4 _____

Current Words

1 _____ 2 _____

3 _____ 4 _____

Sound Alike Words

1 _____ 2 _____

Review Trick Words

1 _____ 2 _____

Sentences

1 _____

_____

2 _____

_____

Sounds

1 _____ 2 _____ 3 _____ 4 _____

Review Words

1 _____ 2 _____

3 _____ 4 _____

Current Words

1 _____ 2 _____

3 _____ 4 _____

Sound Alike Words

1 _____ 2 _____

Review Trick Words

1 _____ 2 _____

Sentences

1 _____

_____

2 _____

_____

Sounds

1 _____ 2 _____ 3 _____ 4 _____

Review Words

1 _____ 2 _____

3 _____ 4 _____

Current Words

1 _____ 2 _____

3 _____ 4 _____

Sound Alike Words

1 _____ 2 _____

Review Trick Words

1 _____ 2 _____

Sentences

1 _____

_____

2 _____

_____

Check-up ☐

Sounds

1 _____ 2 _____ 3 _____ 4 _____

Review Words

1 _____ 2 _____

3 _____ 4 _____

Current Words

1 _____ 2 _____

3 _____ 4 _____

Sound Alike Words

1 _____ 2 _____

Review Trick Words

1 _____ 2 _____

Sentences

1 _____

2 _____

Check-up ☐

Sounds

1   2   3   4

Review Words

1   2

3   4

Current Words

1   2

3   4

Sound Alike Words

1   2

Review Trick Words

1   2

Sentences

1

2

Sounds

1 _____ 2 _____ 3 _____ 4 _____

Review Words

1 _____ 2 _____

3 _____ 4 _____

Current Words

1 _____ 2 _____

3 _____ 4 _____

Sound Alike Words

1 _____ 2 _____

Review Trick Words

1 _____ 2 _____

Sentences

1 _____

_____

2 _____

_____

Sounds

1 _____ 2 _____ 3 _____ 4 _____

Review Words

1 _____ 2 _____

3 _____ 4 _____

Current Words

1 _____ 2 _____

3 _____ 4 _____

Sound Alike Words

1 _____ 2 _____

Review Trick Words

1 _____ 2 _____

Sentences

1

2

Sounds

1   2   3   4

Review Words

1   2

3   4

Current Words

1   2

3   4

Sound Alike Words

1   2

Review Trick Words

1   2

Sentences

1

2

Sounds

1 _____ 2 _____ 3 _____ 4 _____

Review Words

1 _____ 2 _____

3 _____ 4 _____

Current Words

1 _____ 2 _____

3 _____ 4 _____

Sound Alike Words

1 _____ 2 _____

Review Trick Words

1 _____ 2 _____

Sentences

1 _____

_____

2 _____

_____

Sounds

1 _____ 2 _____ 3 _____ 4 _____

Review Words

1 _____ 2 _____

3 _____ 4 _____

Current Words

1 _____ 2 _____

3 _____ 4 _____

Sound Alike Words

1 _____ 2 _____

Review Trick Words

1 _____ 2 _____

Sentences

1 _____

2 _____

Sounds

1 _____ 2 _____ 3 _____ 4 _____

Review Words

1 _____ 2 _____

3 _____ 4 _____

Current Words

1 _____ 2 _____

3 _____ 4 _____

Sound Alike Words

1 _____ 2 _____

Review Trick Words

1 _____ 2 _____

Sentences

1 _____

_____

2 _____

_____

Today's Date: _____ *Check-up* ☐

Sounds

1 _____ 2 _____ 3 _____ 4 _____

Review Words

1 _____ 2 _____

3 _____ 4 _____

Current Words

1 _____ 2 _____

3 _____ 4 _____

Sound Alike Words

1 _____ 2 _____

Review Trick Words

1 _____ 2 _____

Sentences

1 _____

_____

2 _____

_____

Sounds

1 _____ 2 _____

3 _____ 4 _____

Sound Alike Words

1 _____ 2 _____

3 _____ 4 _____

Words

1 _____ 2 _____

3 _____ 4 _____

5 _____

Sentences

1 _____

2 _____

Unit Test Grading

Sounds: _____ / 4	Sound Alike Words: _____ / 4	Score: _____
Words: _____ / 5	Sentences:	x 4
Marking: _____ / 5	Words: _____ / 5	Total Score: _____ / 100
	Trick Words: _____ / 2	

☐ Legibility   ☐ Capitalization   ☐ Punctuation   ☐ Phrasing

Sounds

1   2

3   4

Sound Alike Words

1   2

3   4

Words

1   2

3   4

5

Sentences

1 _____

_____

2 _____

_____

Unit Test Grading		
Sounds: _____ / 4	Sound Alike Words: _____ / 4	Score: _____
Words: _____ / 5	Sentences:	x 4
Marking: _____ / 5	Words: _____ / 5	Total Score: _____ / 100
	Trick Words: _____ / 2	

☐ Legibility   ☐ Capitalization   ☐ Punctuation   ☐ Phrasing

Sounds

1 _____ 2 _____

3 _____ 4 _____

Sound Alike Words

1 _____ 2 _____

3 _____ 4 _____

Words

1 _____ 2 _____

3 _____ 4 _____

5 _____

Sentences

1

2

Unit Test Grading

Sounds: _____ / 4	Sound Alike Words: _____ / 4		Score: _____
Words: _____ / 5	Sentences:		x 4
Marking: _____ / 5	Words: _____ / 5		Total Score: _____ / 100
	Trick Words: _____ / 2		

☐ Legibility ☐ Capitalization ☐ Punctuation ☐ Phrasing

Sounds

1 _____   2 _____

3 _____   4 _____

Sound Alike Words

1 _____   2 _____

3 _____   4 _____

Words

1 _____   2 _____

3 _____   4 _____

5 _____

Sentences

1

2

Unit Test Grading

Sounds: _____ / 4	Sound Alike Words: _____ / 4	Score: _____	
Words: _____ / 5	Sentences:	x 4	
Marking: _____ / 5	Words: _____ / 5	Total Score: _____ / 100	
	Trick Words: _____ / 2		

☐ Legibility   ☐ Capitalization   ☐ Punctuation   ☐ Phrasing

Sounds

1   2

3   4

Sound Alike Words

1   2

3   4

Words

1   2

3   4

5

Sentences

1 _____

2 _____

Unit Test Grading

Sounds: _____ / 4	Sound Alike Words: _____ / 4	Score: _____
Words: _____ / 5	Sentences:	x 4
Marking: _____ / 5	Words: _____ / 5	Total Score: _____ / 100
	Trick Words: _____ / 2	

☐ Legibility ☐ Capitalization ☐ Punctuation ☐ Phrasing

Sounds

1   2

3   4

Sound Alike Words

1   2

3   4

Words

1   2

3   4

5

Sentences

1 _____

_____

2 _____

_____

Unit Test Grading

Sounds: _____ / 4	Sound Alike Words: _____ / 4	Score: _____	
Words: _____ / 5	Sentences:		x 4
Marking: _____ / 5	Words: _____ / 5	Total Score: _____ / 100	
	Trick Words: _____ / 2		

☐ Legibility ☐ Capitalization ☐ Punctuation ☐ Phrasing

Sounds

1 _____ 2 _____

3 _____ 4 _____

Sound Alike Words

1 _____ 2 _____

3 _____ 4 _____

Words

1 _____ 2 _____

3 _____ 4 _____

5 _____

Sentences

1

2

Unit Test Grading

Sounds: _____ / 4	Sound Alike Words: _____ / 4	Score: _____
Words: _____ / 5	Sentences:	x 4
Marking: _____ / 5	Words: _____ / 5	Total Score: _____ / 100
	Trick Words: _____ / 2	

☐ Legibility   ☐ Capitalization   ☐ Punctuation   ☐ Phrasing

Today's Date: *Test for Unit No.* *Page 1*

Sounds

1 2

3 4

Sound Alike Words

1 2

3 4

Words

1 2

3 4

5

Sentences

1 _____

_____

2 _____

_____

Unit Test Grading

Sounds:	_____ / 4	Sound Alike Words:	_____ / 4	Score:	_____
Words:	_____ / 5	Sentences:			x 4
Marking:	_____ / 5	Words:	_____ / 5	Total Score:	_____ / 100
		Trick Words:	_____ / 2		

☐ Legibility   ☐ Capitalization   ☐ Punctuation   ☐ Phrasing

Sounds

1 _____   2 _____

3 _____   4 _____

Sound Alike Words

1 _____   2 _____

3 _____   4 _____

Words

1 _____   2 _____

3 _____   4 _____

5 _____

Sentences

1

2

Unit Test Grading

Sounds: _____ / 4	Sound Alike Words: _____ / 4	Score: _____	
Words: _____ / 5	Sentences:	x 4	
Marking: _____ / 5	Words: _____ / 5	Total Score: _____ / 100	
	Trick Words: _____ / 2		

☐ Legibility   ☐ Capitalization   ☐ Punctuation   ☐ Phrasing

Sounds

1   2

3   4

Sound Alike Words

1   2

3   4

Words

1   2

3   4

5

Sentences

1 _____

_____

_____

2 _____

_____

_____

Unit Test Grading

Sounds: _____ / 4	Sound Alike Words: _____ / 4	Score: _____	
Words: _____ / 5	Sentences:	x 4	
Marking: _____ / 5	Words: _____ / 5	Total Score: _____ / 100	
	Trick Words: _____ / 2		

☐ Legibility   ☐ Capitalization   ☐ Punctuation   ☐ Phrasing

Sounds

1 _____   2 _____

3 _____   4 _____

Sound Alike Words

1 _____   2 _____

3 _____   4 _____

Words

1 _____   2 _____

3 _____   4 _____

5 _____

Sentences

_1_ _____

_____

_2_ _____

_____

Unit Test Grading

Sounds: _____ / 4	Sound Alike Words: _____ / 4	Score: _____	
Words: _____ / 5	Sentences:		
Marking: _____ / 5	Words: _____ / 5	Total Score: _____ / 100	x 4
	Trick Words: _____ / 2		

☐ Legibility   ☐ Capitalization   ☐ Punctuation   ☐ Phrasing

Sounds

1   2

3   4

Sound Alike Words

1   2

3   4

Words

1   2

3   4

5

Sentences

1 _____

2 _____

Unit Test Grading

Sounds: _____ / 4	Sound Alike Words: _____ / 4		Score: _____	
Words: _____ / 5	Sentences:		x 4	
Marking: _____ / 5	Words: _____ / 5		Total Score: _____ / 100	
	Trick Words: _____ / 2			

☐ Legibility ☐ Capitalization ☐ Punctuation ☐ Phrasing

Sounds

1   2

3   4

Sound Alike Words

1   2

3   4

Words

1   2

3   4

5

Sentences

1

2

Unit Test Grading

Sounds: _____ / 4	Sound Alike Words: _____ / 4		Score: _____	
Words: _____ / 5	Sentences:		x 4	
Marking: _____ / 5	Words: _____ / 5		Total Score: _____ / 100	
	Trick Words: _____ / 2			

☐ Legibility   ☐ Capitalization   ☐ Punctuation   ☐ Phrasing

Sounds

1   2

3   4

Sound Alike Words

1   2

3   4

Words

1   2

3   4

5

Sentences

1 _____

_____

2 _____

_____

Unit Test Grading

Sounds: _____ / 4	Sound Alike Words: _____ / 4	Score: _____
Words: _____ / 5	Sentences:	x 4
Marking: _____ / 5	Words: _____ / 5	Total Score: _____ / 100
	Trick Words: _____ / 2	

☐ Legibility   ☐ Capitalization   ☐ Punctuation   ☐ Phrasing

Sounds

1 _____   2 _____

3 _____   4 _____

Sound Alike Words

1 _____   2 _____

3 _____   4 _____

Words

1 _____   2 _____

3 _____   4 _____

5 _____

Sentences

1 _____

_____

2 _____

_____

_____

Unit Test Grading

Sounds: _____ / 4   Sound Alike Words: _____ / 4   Score: _____

Words: _____ / 5   Sentences: x 4

Marking: _____ / 5   Words: _____ / 5   Total Score: _____ / 100

Trick Words: _____ / 2

☐ Legibility   ☐ Capitalization   ☐ Punctuation   ☐ Phrasing

Sounds

1 _____ 2 _____

3 _____ 4 _____

Sound Alike Words

1 _____ 2 _____

3 _____ 4 _____

Words

1 _____ 2 _____

3 _____ 4 _____

5 _____

Sentences

1 _____

_____

_____

2 _____

_____

_____

Unit Test Grading

Sounds: _____ / 4	Sound Alike Words: _____ / 4		Score: _____	
Words: _____ / 5	Sentences:		x 4	
Marking: _____ / 5	Words: _____ / 5		Total Score: _____ / 100	
	Trick Words: _____ / 2			

☐ Legibility   ☐ Capitalization   ☐ Punctuation   ☐ Phrasing

Sounds

1 _____   2 _____

3 _____   4 _____

Sound Alike Words

1 _____   2 _____

3 _____   4 _____

Words

1 _____   2 _____

3 _____   4 _____

5 _____

Sentences

1

2

Unit Test Grading

Sounds: _____ / 4	Sound Alike Words: _____ / 4	Score: _____	
Words: _____ / 5	Sentences:	x 4	
Marking: _____ / 5	Words: _____ / 5	Total Score: _____ / 100	
	Trick Words: _____ / 2		

☐ Legibility   ☐ Capitalization   ☐ Punctuation   ☐ Phrasing

Sounds

1   2

3   4

Sound Alike Words

1   2

3   4

Words

1   2

3   4

5

Sentences

1 _____

_____

_____

_____

2 _____

_____

_____

_____

Unit Test Grading

Sounds: _____ / 4	Sound Alike Words: _____ / 4	Score: _____
Words: _____ / 5	Sentences:	x 4
Marking: _____ / 5	Words: _____ / 5	Total Score: _____ / 100
	Trick Words: _____ / 2	

☐ Legibility   ☐ Capitalization   ☐ Punctuation   ☐ Phrasing

Sounds

1 _____ 2 _____

3 _____ 4 _____

Sound Alike Words

1 _____ 2 _____

3 _____ 4 _____

Words

1 _____ 2 _____

3 _____ 4 _____

5 _____

Sentences

1

2

Unit Test Grading

Sounds: _____ / 4	Sound Alike Words: _____ / 4	Score: _____	
Words: _____ / 5	Sentences:	x 4	
Marking: _____ / 5	Words: _____ / 5	Total Score: _____ / 100	
	Trick Words: _____ / 2		

☐ Legibility   ☐ Capitalization   ☐ Punctuation   ☐ Phrasing

Sounds

1 _____   2 _____

3 _____   4 _____

Sound Alike Words

1 _____   2 _____

3 _____   4 _____

Words

1 _____   2 _____

3 _____   4 _____

5 _____

Sentences

1

2

Unit Test Grading			

Sounds: _____ / 4   Sound Alike Words: _____ / 4

Words: _____ / 5   Sentences:

Marking: _____ / 5   Words: _____ / 5

Trick Words: _____ / 2

Score: _____

x 4

Total Score: _____ / 100

☐ Legibility   ☐ Capitalization   ☐ Punctuation   ☐ Phrasing

NOTES

Capitalization and Punctuation

 Capital Letters

A B C D E F
G H I J K L
M N O P Q R S
T U V W X Y Z

 Capitalization

- Beginning of sentence: <u>T</u>he dog is cute.
- People's names: <u>J</u>ohn and <u>M</u>aria are here.
- Specific names of places: <u>L</u>ong <u>P</u>ond, <u>W</u>isconsin
- Days of the week, months of the year: <u>F</u>riday, <u>J</u>une
- Beginning word in quote: Mr. Smith said, "<u>Y</u>es, I will go!"

Punctuation

- Period (**.**): I am six years old.
- Question Mark (**?**): When will you visit?
- Exclamation Point (**!**): I love this class!

Other:

- Comma (**,**): September 1, 2012
- Quotes (**" "**): She asked, "How are you?"

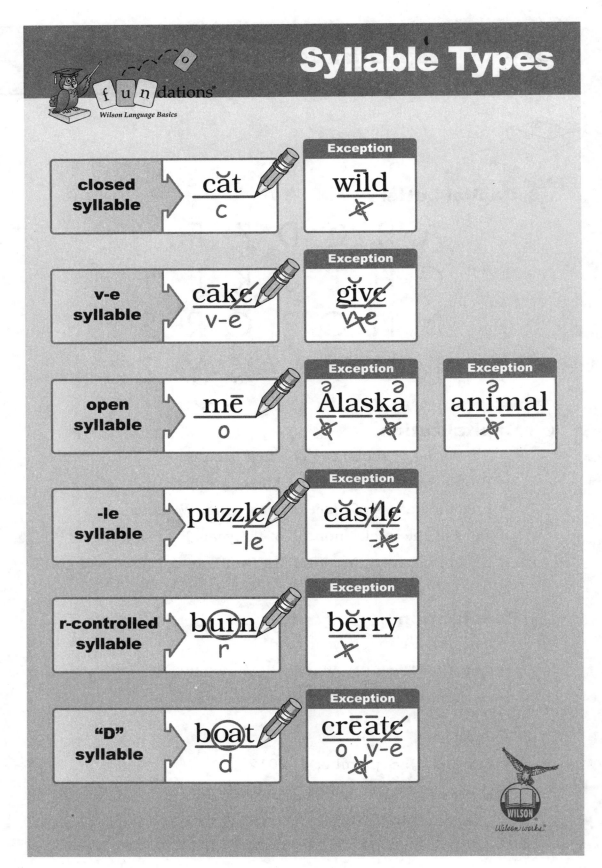

fun dations®
Wilson Language Basics

		Exception
closed syllable	căt / c	wĭld
v-e syllable	cāke / v-e	gĭve / v-e
open syllable	mē / o	Alaska (Exception) · animal (Exception)
-le syllable	puzzle / -le	căstle / -le
r-controlled syllable	burn / r	bĕrry
"D" syllable	boat / d	crēate / o / v-e